D1016973

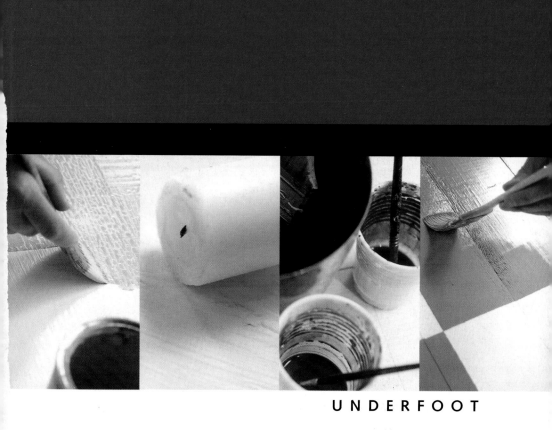

U N D E R F O O T

UNDER

Original photography by
Marie-Louise Avery and Sue Baker

JOCASTA INNES AROUND THE HOUSE

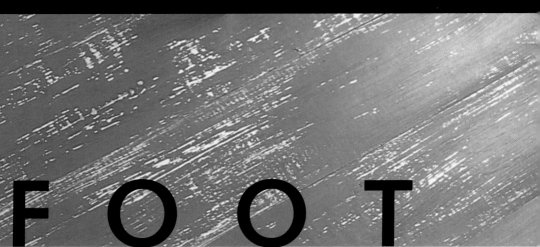

F O O T

Text by JUDY SPOURS

A Bulfinch Press Book
Little, Brown and Company
Boston New York Toronto London

AROUND THE HOUSE is intended as a series that will expand into a whole shelf of stylish, practical and focussed handbooks for home decorators. Small enough to be affordable, but long enough to deal with their subjects in depth, they will offer a generous choice of hands-on projects, clearly explained and amplified by excellent, specially-commissioned photographs. If cooks can buy small, subject-specific books such as Pasta, Soups and Salads, why shouldn't decorators be offered the same approach, and choice?

I believe this series – something of a publishing 'first' – will encourage a radical re-think of decorating books, their treatment, format and presentation.

Watch this space!

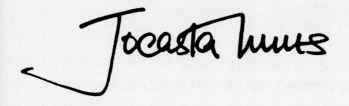

CONTENTS

6   Introduction: A Brief History of Floors
24   Preparation: Making Good and Squaring Off

28   THE PROJECTS
30   Paints and Varnishes
   35   Classic White Floor
   36   Scandinavian Bleached Floor
   41   Subtle Crackle-Glazed Floor
   45   Denim-Look Floor
   48   Floral Floor Tiles
   53   Floor Cloth: Homage to the Nineteenth
       Century
   56   *Faux* Parquetry Floor
   61   Gingham-Look Floor
   64   Modern Mosaic Floor
   69   Stencilled Mosaic Floor
   73   Chequerboard Floor
   76   Combed Floor
   81   Patchwork Tile Doorstep

84   Maintenance and Cleaning
90   Further Reading
91   Stencil Templates
94   Paint Magic Shops
96   Acknowledgements and Picture Credits

INTRODUCTION

A BRIEF HISTORY OF FLOORS

Way back in 1880, in a lecture delivered to the Society of Arts in London, the architect Robert W. Edis declaimed on the subject of fitted carpets: *It is a matter of astonishment to me that there are still a large number of people who are content to keep this exceedingly bad arrangement of floor covering, and who object altogether to having a certain amount of plain floor space all around the sides of the room. In the first place, this covering of the whole surface is unhealthy; in the second place, it is dirty; and, in the third place, the cost of the carpet is infinitely more than the cost of painting or staining the edges of the rooms.*

He could have been talking in 1980, with more intense decorative despair, when he would still have encountered fitted carpets everywhere — although they would have been less filthy as a result of the invention of the vacuum cleaner. Today, however, tastes are beginning to swing back to an interest in carpetless floors, to the types of hard coverings perfected in continental Europe and those used extensively in Britain and America 150 years ago and more — bare boards, tiles, stone, mosaics. And as global warming hots up, surely a preference for cosy carpets will be further overtaken by a desire for some-

A return to the flooring of the past: a modern interpretation of a traditional parquet floor, using timber as a veneer.

thing cooler underfoot, even in the northern hemisphere.

The text and projects in this book give ideas and methods for many different effects that are suitable for domestic floors. In some projects, painting and staining imitate otherwise expensive or impractical surfaces. Others are inspired by the skills of craftspeople of the past, even — in the case of mosaics — those of antiquity. Yet more are up-to-the-minute effects accomplished with new products. It is fascinating to delve into

A detail from a mosaic pavement in Pompeii, showing a gentle and humorous *cave canem* dog pattern.

the history of floor designs, to understand how and why various materials were used, not just in grand country houses but also in workers' cottages or suburban houses, and how those materials were modified and added to over the centuries. The story of floors is, curiously, largely ignored in histories of interior design, which prefer to concentrate instead on walls, ceilings and furnishings. Yet the floor should be a primary preoccupation when decorating, as it often was in earlier centuries. After all, it occupies an enormous proportion of open space in any room and can make or break an overall design.

The Ancients Roman architects had a clear understanding of the decorative value of the floor, which would be a particularly strong focus in sparsely furnished rooms. Perhaps the idea of mosaic came to mind when an early designer dreamed about the pleasing effect of different coloured pebbles on a beach; in any event, wherever stone of tolerable hardness and two colours, or shades of one colour, was found, there the chief material for mosaic was ready to be exploited.

The Romans developed mosaic floors to exquisite and complex heights, inventing different styles and stone-cutting methods to produce a wide variety of effects.

The most basic, tesselated, floors consisted of small pieces of marble cut into cubes about an inch square; sectile floors featured slices across the grain of marble; the most sophisticated, *opus vermiculatum*, were composed of sinuous figures and landscapes in exact naturalistic colours and imitated wall paintings.

The colours came from different stones. In Romano-British mosaics, for example, white and cream were found in chalk and limestone; reds and oranges in clay bricks and tiles; blues, blacks and greys in Purbeck marble and shale. The results could be spectacular. When Pompeii was excavated, a floor mosaic of extraordinary detail, accuracy and colour was

Mosaics old and new: detail of a Venetian marble pavement (top); ceramic 'laid by the yard' mosaic in an urban bathroom (above); and pebbles in graduated sizes marking out a knot pattern in a modern garden (right).

revealed in the House of Faun. It depicts twelve horses, twenty-two people and an enormous water chariot. All this from stone found in the surrounding landscape and stuck down with a cement made out of slaked lime and powdered marble which was blended with water and whites of eggs.

Other mosaics simply exploited uncut pebbles of varying sizes, characteristically grey pebbles inlaid with abstract or naturalistic designs of white pebbles. These were often used in exterior living areas — courtyards, patios, entranceways.

Enamelled tiles were produced in ancient Egypt and Babylon, and the art spread eastwards to Persia where tile decoration developed to an inimitable level. At Isfahan, for example, the colours in a tiled floor dating from 1690 reflect and complement the wall decoration, demonstrating skills which are still in use today.

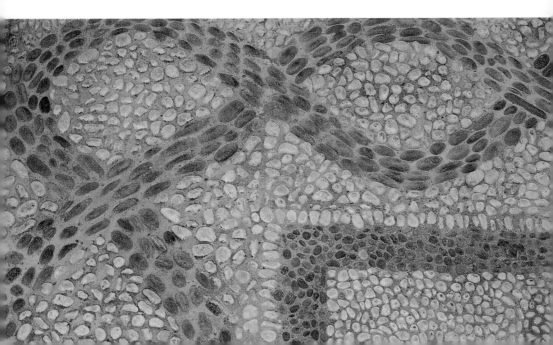

Mud The cheapest, easiest material to hand for flooring was bare earth, and beaten mud floors are timeless and universal, persisting into the twentieth century in parts of the world. They require the earth to be dug, raked into small grains and mixed with water until it is as soft as mortar. The mud is piled onto the ground of a cottage, left for two weeks, then beaten smooth with broad, flat pieces of wood. Any faults in the surface are mended later with clay or earth, used in exactly the same way as a proprietary filler.

Sometimes the mud surface is strengthened by incorporating bones to hold it together, and on occasion these are carefully arranged to make patterns on the floor. Ox blood mixed with the mud gives a much smoother surface and a pleasing russet colour. The floor is then strewn with rushes or straw to absorb dirt and moisture and to make it softer to walk on.

In many a medieval house the mud floor was less than salubrious. The rushes were rarely replaced, and among them would lie the debris of everyday life — grease, fragments of food and bones, even animal excrement. The nastiness was sometimes relieved by a scattering of aromatic herbs like lavender and rosemary, but hygiene was low on the medieval agenda. Rushes created dust and pollen and the problem could be dealt with by regularly watering down the floor. In some parts of Britain, a special earthenware watering can was made solely for this purpose.

By the sixteenth century, some cottagers had become more house-proud, and used decorative ideas which developed and persisted into the nineteenth century. Sometimes coloured sands were strewn over the mud, and the sand was even arranged into patterns across the surface, an art form particularly prevalent in Wales. Sand was also later used for 'dry' cleaning floors (see page 86), and was delivered to households all over the country by the sandman.

A humble mud-floored dwelling might nevertheless have had a stone hearth and a stone doorstep. These grander areas of flooring were those onto which the housewife concentrated her artistic imagination and pride. They were decorated with freehand patterns drawn in chalk or with white pipe clay. Characteristic designs developed in different areas of Britain. Infinite patience was no doubt required: the decorations on the doorstep, at least, must have disappeared regularly under the trudge of heavy boots.

In many parts of India mud floors were and still are decorated in almost equal measure to the mud walls of modest houses. The decorations have more than an aesthetic function: they frequently fulfil a sacred or protective role and may mark the seasons of the year or specific festivals. Some are narrative, figurative works, perhaps depicting the cooking of a feast, animals or human figures. Those painted on mud floors with powder paints at harvest time — the new year of the sun in the northern hemisphere — are an example. More everyday, abstract work is regularly done by women, who finger-daub with paint, or even rice paste. Again, these devices are ephemeral, and the march of feet soon obliterates the ingenious work.

Europe and Britain before 1600 From the sixteenth century onwards, decorative paving was widely used in Italy, Germany and France — local freestone was set in a mortar of lime and sand. Pitched stone — cut and rammed down into earth — was also arranged to form patterns, sometimes interspersed with white stones to give a very attractive effect. Even so, the surface was hard underfoot and tended to be cold, damp and comfortless in largely unheated houses: although stone holds heat for a considerable time, it has to acquire it in the first place. Slate was used as a dryer alternative when it was available locally.

In Britain, cottages still had mud floors; it was only grander buildings, such as castles, that possessed properly constructed ones. These may have been of brick, cobbles, clay mixed with fine ash or, rarely, a type of plaster made from lime dust mixed in with clay. An example of this can be seen on the first floor of Hardwick Hall in Derbyshire, the Tudor 'prodigy house' built by Bess of Hardwick. Any warmth or comfort underfoot would at best be provided by the occasional fur or, by Tudor times, rush matting or 'fledges', more sophisticated mats woven in simple, herringbone patterns. The houses also flaunted thin-cut paving stones on the ground floors with oak boards, polished and otherwise unadorned, on the floors above. Stone was seldom used as the indigenous varieties tend to be soft and therefore wear quickly. It was often restricted to the domestic areas — such as kitchens and hallways — of larger houses, where appearance was relatively unimportant.

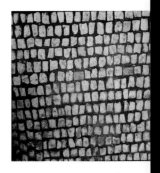

A brick kitchen floor, never out of fashion (right), and granite setts, still fresh after centuries, in a street in Prague (below).

Early paintings of domestic interiors show a fascinating array of floor coverings, often painted with great verisimilitude and therefore providing important historical detail. The fired clay tiles — often in black and white, sometimes in buff and blue — of Dutch interiors are perhaps the most familiar. A selection of paintings from the fifteenth century, for example, shows a variety of floors: richly patterned ornamental tiles in a Flemish work; a French miniature with wall-to-wall rush matting; and an extraordinary and delightful German painting of a young woman in a room of light, wood boards scattered with scented wild flowers.

Brick, tile and mosaic paving was common in Europe throughout the Middle Ages, and even reached some grander houses in England. Clay tiles were inlaid into

floors in simple mosaic patterns and were coloured with muted natural dyes, or wooden-stamped and the impressions filled in with clay of another colour. Upper rooms had timber floors, made from oak or the lighter elm, which formed the ceilings of the rooms below — sometimes complex wooden structures that accommodated elaborately painted decorations.

Pattern books full of designs for floors were published in Europe in the fifteenth and sixteenth centuries, but were taken up in Britain only in the early seventeenth century, when floors were given serious stylistic attention.

Wood Until the middle of the eighteenth century, beautiful wooden floorboards were intended to be seen, not covered over with rugs or carpets. Wide oak boards were used in the best rooms, and by the mid-seventeenth century deal (fir) was imported into Britain from Scandinavia and used in less important ones. By the late eighteenth century the status of household areas could be deduced from the flooring: oak in the parlour; deal in the bedrooms; elm in the servants' garrets; and stone in the dairy. In northern Europe, floorboards were arranged in decorative patterns early on in the seventeenth century, but in Britain wooden floors remained plain until the introduction of parquetry in the middle of the century.

Wood-block floors in antique French oak laid (left) in a popular nineteenth-century herringbone pattern, and (right) as a squared grid desiged for a seventeenth-century château.

Parquetry floors consisted of different types of woods, tongued and grooved into geometrical patterns of varying hues. They could incorporate a variety of woods such as oak or cedar inlaid with walnut, yew, mahogany, box or ebony. By the late eighteenth century machine-cut, very thin strips of

wood arranged in patterns on a canvas backing formed 'carpet parquetry'. This could be laid either as a border or as an entire floor without interfering with the old surface and requiring much less labour to instal.

The same period also saw a vogue for painted floors, boards decorated with geometric patterns or stencilled with flowers or leaves. Even earlier, unglamorous wooden floors were painted in imitation of another material: black and white to copy tiles; black, brown and red to simulate parquetry or inlaid marble.

Stone, Marble and Scagliola In Britain Inigo Jones (1573–1652) began a classical reaction against Jacobean decorative exuberance. He designed the first truly classical floor, of radiating black and white stone, for the cubic hall in the Queen's House at Greenwich in London. Built between 1616 and 1635, the house was England's first Italianate villa.

A black and white chequered design was the commonest pattern for floors made from marble in the seventeenth century, black and white octagons in the eighteenth. In very grand houses, marble floors could be much more elaborate and polychromatic; they often complemented walls, marble pillars and ceilings and were an important element in the decorative unity of a room.

Hard-wearing and expensive, marble was also cold and austere. In seventeenth-century Italy *scagliola* was invented as a cheaper (though less durable) alternative to the real thing. Proper *scagliola* was a composition of gypsum, glue and colours and sometimes incorporated chips of real marble — in effect, it was a rather special polished concrete. Some so-called *scagliola* floors were actually made of stucco, or plaster, beaten and stiffened with other ingredients. If badly applied this was likely to crack as it dried. *Scagliola* was used to imitate marble walls, ceilings

and columns as well as floors, and at its best created a marvellously authentic look of real marble, or compelling fantasies of invented marbles that could not be found in nature.

The Rise and Rise of the Floor Cloth   Now more commonly used to describe an old dishcloth demoted to clean the floor, the words 'floor cloth' once applied to something of much more aesthetic interest. From the early eighteenth century, floor cloths were one of the most versatile and practical of floor coverings. They were made from seamless, widths of coarse canvas (often manufactured on the coast adjacent to sail makers) stretched and stiffened with size to produce a smooth surface. Both sides were then painted with many coats of linseed oil — hence the alternative name 'oil cloth'. A floor cloth could be painted in one colour or decorated with block printing, stencilling or freehand patterns. This design versatility — its ability to fulfil any decorative fantasy — together with the fact that it was waterproof and easily cleaned, accounts for its enduring popularity right up until this century.

Throughout the eighteenth century, for example, the excavation of Roman pavements made mosaic designs a 'must' in fashionable houses. A floor cloth decorated with block printing that imitated mosaic was an easy and cheap alternative to the (hugely expensive) real thing. Other examples copied marble or parquetry floors or the patterned Turkey carpets which were also becoming fashionable. By the nineteenth century, however, the designs had become overblown, compelling Charles Eastlake, in his didactic and

Part of an *opus sectile* sliced marble pavement in the cathedral on Torcello, in the Venetian lagoon (left) and a corner of our recreated floorcloth (above); see page 53.

somewhat humourless *Hints on Household Taste* of 1878, to comment that 'the most tasteful should be geometric patterns in no more than two colours, or, better, two tints of the same colour'. We have borne his advice in mind when designing our own, relatively austere, floor cloth on page 53.

Floor cloths were made until the early years of this century, but their decline was inevitable after the invention of a better alternative: linoleum — thick, pulverized cork and resin on a strong canvas backing — was patented in 1860. Its hardwearing surface was ideally suited to a printed pattern, and lino was consistently used until its cheapness and decorative predictability caused it to fall from favour in the second half of the twentieth century.

Nineteenth-Century Town and Country By the late nineteenth century the floor of a cottage might have graduated from mud to brick or undecorated earthenware tiles. Bricks were laid flat or on edge and embedded in sand or mortar. Even so, Seebohm Rowntree, in his early sociological study *How the Labourer Lives*, published in 1913, commented that 'brick floors … looked extremely comfortless'. Better-off cottagers had strips of coconut matting here and there, or maybe a homemade 'paper' carpet, woven from linen, gauze or coarse cloth rags. The poorer would merely throw down a potato or corn sack as a hearth rug.

The women of cottage households continued the decorative tradition of enhancing their humble floors by making patterns, particularly on flagged stone, with 'rubbing stones'. The basic designs were handed down through the generations — for instance, broad white lines drawn with limestone or sandstone around the edges of a room, or simple twisted flourishes in its centre. Some patterns were more complex: a circle in the centre with corresponding circles at the edges; looped lines across the room diagonals; or a series of lozenge shapes. Colours were provided by other readily available natural materials: brownstone, particularly in Yorkshire, or soot mixed with water to make a shiny black surface.

Meanwhile, more concerned with the homes of the emerging middle class, Eastlake proposed that 'the best way of treating a hall floor in town or country is to pave it with encaustic tiles'. From the 1830s tiles treated with elaborate patterns or simple geometrics were produced in the potteries of England, most famously by Minton. In the United States, ornamental floor tiles were pioneered by Samuel Keys from 1871 at his Star Encaustic Tile Company in Pittsburgh, where he produced both plain and patterned vitreous tiles. Such mass-production enabled many households to commission complex patterns, perhaps with tiles radiating in a circular pattern from the centre of a room, with a Turkey or Wilton carpet proudly displayed in the middle.

Elsewhere in America, Shaker interiors of the middle of the nineteenth century were characterized by simple wood boards, left bare or painted white, and often partly covered by an oval, patterned rush mat. A similar style was current in nineteenth-century Scandinavia — pale boards with simple, flat-weave rugs with stripes or geometric designs. In central and southern Europe chequered or other geometric tiles, most often black and white, were the norm in modestly sophisticated houses anywhere from Italy to Poland.

Into the Twentieth Century At the start of the twentieth century old flooring habits (and design pundits' edicts) died hard in Britain. C. F. A. Voysey (1857–1941) instructed the owners of small country houses: 'Construct your hall floor with large flags of stone or marble, slate or brick. If the floor be carpeted and the weather dirty, it is discomforting to sensitive creatures with cleanly habits.' Less 'sensitive creatures' still had to make do with brick, boards and even — in the poorest homes — mud, and remain immune to the finer points of bad weather.

Elsewhere, the growing Edwardian suburbs were characterized by houses whose living rooms had floors of polished boards scattered with rugs or mats, as fine as could be afforded. The kitchen or scullery would be wall-to-wall

York stone flags laid in a hallway, giving out onto a mosaic doorstep made of broken ceramic tiles.

linoleum, usually of one colour and unpatterned, cheered up, perhaps, by a brightly coloured rug. There was also a fashion for coconut matting on the kitchen floor, but this was found to be unhygienic as it was difficult to remove grease and other stains.

Fashions were not that different elsewhere in the Western world. A rural kitchen in America would probably have a floor of wooden boards, decorated with a simple oval rush mat or striped textile rug. In Sweden, floorboards might be painted with a simple geometric design; in Denmark they might be whitened and then distressed to give a light and airy appearance.

As the century continued, floor design in the average home seemed to be of less and less interest to its occupants and inspired little or no invention. Ubiquitous fitted carpets covered the floors of British houses; pale wood blocks or parquetry those of Scandinavia; terracotta tiles were everywhere, indoors and out, across southern Europe. Designers may have experimented with the new and unusual in grander houses and public buildings — with parti-coloured rubber compositions, bold and contrasting geometric tiles, marble strips combined with brick, marbled lino mosaicized into classical designs, three-ply waxed birchwood, 'carpet' painted onto the floorboards — but such adventures rarely found their way through the door of an ordinary house. Choosing new carpet colours and laying something bland and waterproof in kitchen and bathroom (unless that too was supplied with fitted carpet) were the major flooring concerns of the British home decorator.

As our knowledge of, and appetite for, interiors ideas of the past and present develop late in this century, and as materials become more technically advanced and practicable, enthusiasm for a huge variety of different hard-floor surfaces is emerging. In particular, the cosiness of the fitted carpet, once an essential in a 'cold' climate, is becoming irrelevant in competently heated, double-glazed houses. In many homes bare floorboards are scattered with oriental rugs or kilims, or their cheaper alternatives, while jute, sisal, coir, seagrass, or even hemp, are starting to replace wool and nylon for wall-to-wall coverings.

A wonderful variety of materials is now available for hard flooring, some very expensive, others less so, and many effects can imitate a grand style cheaply and comparatively easily, as the projects in this book show. Encouragingly, too, commercial designs are increasingly international and home decorators today can combine and experiment with the best ideas from a variety of cultures. Stone flooring comes in the form of Venetian marble, limestone, slate of many colours and textures, and sandstone, a particularly hard-wearing product. Terracotta tiles are produced in an enormous range of shades and shapes, and can be combined with more expensive and decorative encaustic tiles. These, in turn, may be plain, patterned, crackle-glazed or copies of medieval, Dutch, Mediterranean or Islamic designs. In some recent examples the pattern is inlaid and embossed on the tile before it is fired, then smoothed to produce a mosaic rather than painted effect. For exterior use, encaustic tiles can be glazed to look like stone and treated to resist frost.

Wood floors may be polished, painted, distressed or woodstained boards or parquet blocks, hardwood strips or tongue-and-groove in woods that provide different shades of colour and grain to complement different decorative schemes — oak, ash, pine, maple, birch, beech, cherry, spruce. If you can afford them, mosaics are still cut by hand and laid by artists, and are becoming increasingly popular, as are their *trompe l'oeil* imitations. Some suppliers produce mosaics that are ready to be laid in strips. Geometric or naturalistic patterns of stones and marble cobbles, even resilient sea shells, can be set in concrete floors, both indoors and out. Terrazzo — granite or marble chips mixed with concrete or resins and ground smooth — is an enduringly popular composite for floors that would have been marble centuries ago. Anyone who wants an antique surface can acquire and re-lay the real thing as 'reclaimed' flagstones and oak boards are lifted from one building and imposed on another.

Vinyl floorings can be astonishingly versatile, as shown in these three stunning examples: subtly contrasting wood finishes (above left); an octagonal centrepiece in beech, maple, rosewood and teak (above right); and a wonderful Adamesque classical floor cut from multi-coloured vinyl tiles (opposite).

Technological developments in the manufacture of linoleum, and its synthetic cousin vinyl, have revived their popularity. Lino may be marbled or left to show off its natural components. Vinyl can be compressed to look like cork or brick, marble or slate without their coldness underfoot, and cushioned for greater comfort and warmth. It can also look wonderful, with no pretence of imitating another material, in startlingly bright colours and smooth finishes. Sheet vinyl can be cut and inlaid to produce any pattern provided the artist is adept enough; tiles can be laid as a chequerboard or kaleidoscope of different coloured squares, or cut and juxtaposed into simple, geometric patterns.

Rubber is hard-wearing and is available in relief-patterned tiles. Cork tiles are cheap and look beautiful when they are waxed rather than varnished with acrylic. Even if a floor is completely plain, it takes little cost or effort to enhance it with an occasional mosaic inset or a border of glazed tiles. And, as a number of our projects show, any of the grander hard surfaces can be amusingly imitated, given a *trompe l'oeil* treatment with a pot or two of paint deftly applied to old floorboards.

Robert W. Edis, he of the 1880 lecture to the Society of Arts, might have been happy after all at the end of the twentieth century, encountering flooring soul-mates who would agree vehemently with his distaste for 'the evil of fixed carpets' and his faith in the beauty and versatility of hard floor surfaces.

PREPARATION

MAKING GOOD

No one would demand that a floor surface be as smooth and flawless as a wall or ceiling, particularly as it does not dictate the same sort of critical perspective to a finished room as these other 'flat' surfaces. Paint finishes can be applied to relatively uneven floors and still look the part, but mosaics or woodstain finishes need a fairly level base in order to be successful. In any case, it is best to make sure that the floor surface is as good as it can be without major expense.

The chances are that when you move into a new house or take up old carpets and underfelt, you will find floorboards which may be covered with hardboard, chipboard or medium-density fibre board (MDF) sheets. Loose floorboards certainly need to be firmly nailed down, and damaged ones with splits or large nail holes should be replaced, ideally with boards of a similar age. Other holes or indentations can be filled with a proprietary wood filler. If the floorboards are covered with any of the above products these must be well laid to provide a smooth surface for any effect. If there are large gaps, consider relaying or putting another layer over them.

If a floor has been painted or varnished, you may need to remove the old applications, either with a caustic stripper or by sanding the boards with an industrial floor sander. This can readily be hired. Sanding is a messy job and should be done before you start any other decorating as it creates tenacious dust.

Concrete floors are either new or full of craters need to be levelled off with a finer concrete screed which is floated on over the top and settles and dries level, filling in the holes. Beware of doing it yourself: screeding is hard and heavy work. If you are thinking of taking on the task, consult a builder or a good DIY home-improvement manual. Before painting onto concrete, seal with a primer.

CHOOSING A PROJECT FOR YOUR FLOOR

FLOOR EFFECT	YOUR FLOOR SURFACE				
	CEMENT	HARD VINYL	PLANKS	HARDBOARD	CERAMIC TILES
Classic White	✓	✓	✓		
Scandinavian Bleaching			✓		
Subtle Crackle-Glazing		✓	✓	✓	
Denim Look	✓		✓	✓	
Floral 'Tiles'	✓	✓	✓	✓	✓
Floor Cloth	✓	✓	✓	✓	✓
Faux Parquetry			✓	✓	
Gingham Look	✓	✓	✓	✓	
Modern Mosaic	✓	✓		✓	✓
Stencilled Mosaic	✓	✓	✓	✓	
Chequerboard	✓	✓	✓	✓	
Combing	✓	✓	✓	✓	
Patchwork Tiling	✓				✓

IMPORTANT NOTES: Boards can be fixed over concrete, vinyl or small tiled areas to provide a more versatile surface, suitable for any of the projects indicated for hardboard floor surfaces. If you are tiling over ceramic tiles, these should be sound and in good condition, and the surface area fairly limited – it is preferable to remove the tiles first and make good, or board over. Hard vinyl surfaces should be primed well before painting, and the finished effect vanished well before use. DO NOT paint over cushioned vinyl – remove or board over.

S Q U A R I N G   O F F

A number of the step-by-step projects on the following pages rely on geometry for their effects. It is essential that this is exact – a room of chequerboard squares, for instance, will not look good unless the lines are absolutely straight and start from the central point of the room.

If stencils are to be painted at regular intervals across the surface, you will need to mark up the floor in the same way as you would if you were actually painting squares – you then have an easy indication of where to place each stencil, and can remove the chalk lines afterwards.

A very large room will visually accommodate much larger squares than a small one, where they will look better if they are on a smaller scale. This is the first decision you need to make and may also be dictated by the amount of effort you want to put into your project. Generally speaking, the more squares there are the more time they will take to draw up and paint. It is a good idea to make a scaled drawing on graph paper as it gives an accurate impression of how a certain scale of chequer will look in the finished room. If you prepare several scaled drawings with different-sized squares you will be able to make a good decision. It is worth spending time on this planning stage.

Measuring and marking up is boring, but essential. Don't apply a stroke of paint or stick down a single tessera until you are sure you have got it right. You will regret it if you do. What could be a sophisticated imitation of black and white marble or an authentic Roman pavement could become a disappointing mess.

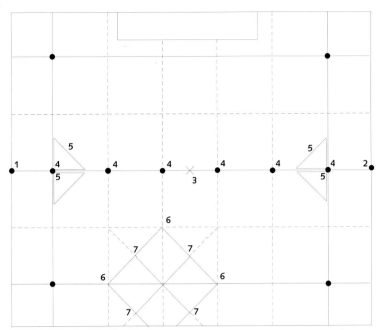

1 To square off the floor, first measure two opposite walls and mark the centre point of each (don't assume they are necessarily of identical length).

2 Stretch a string between the points on the walls and then mark the line it makes along the floor with chalk.

3 The centre of this chalked line is the centre of the room and you need to mark it and remain aware of it.

4 The central point is where you should start with your design, whether it is a stencil, chequer or stripe. Start marking off the width of squares along the existing line until you reach as near as possible to the edges of the room.

5 Then, using a set square, fix four right angles at these furthest width points of the squares. Draw a straight chalk line along these, joining the other two walls with a

straight line. Repeat steps 4 and 5 until you have a square drawn some inches from the edge right round the border of the room, with a central line and template widths marked. Now you can go ahead and fill in all the squares from this grid with the template.

There will always be an irregular space – unless the walls themselves are absolutely square, which is very unlikely – and it is important that this is at the edges of

the room. If you were to start drawing squares along one (not straight) wall, your final pattern would waver drunkenly across the expanse of floor.

6 Arranging the squares on the diagonal, at a 45 degree angle to the boards, can look much more exciting than trying to follow the lines of boards. In any case, this type of effect is designed to disguise the fact that there are floorboards underneath and to imitate a stone or marble surface, and painting diagonally will make the lines of the boards less apparent. If you decide to do this, draw up the floor as above with squares and then, perhaps using a different coloured chalk to avoid confusion, draw diagonal lines across each square to create new squares – the ones that are actually going to be painted.

7 For smaller squares, draw one more set of diagonals.

THE

PROJECTS

Here are step-by-step instructions for floor surfaces that are relatively simple to achieve. Some are designed to create innovative effects, while others imitate styles which have been in existence for centuries — even millennia.

PAINTS AND VARNISHES

Paints and varnishes used in the projects were supplied by the Paint Magic shops, a list of which is given on page 91. Other comparable products can, of course, be used, and you may wish to substitute different colours. Our choice (with the Paint Magic names in brackets) is only a suggestion.

Most of the painted-floor projects are protected by a number of coats of oil-based polyurethane varnish. Very tough and hard-wearing, it dries slowly, is slightly yellowish, and tends to yellow more with time. Elsewhere we have suggested using a water-based acrylic one — or given you a choice between the two. The beauty of an acrylic varnish is that it dries quickly to a clear finish and allows the floor to wear more naturally. Some paint rubs off and the overall effect is eventually of an aged and distressed surface which is in many ways more satisfying than one preserved in

the amber of polyurethane. Two of the projects use white polish, a fast-drying traditional spirit-based varnish as a barrier between the effect and the finishing varnish.

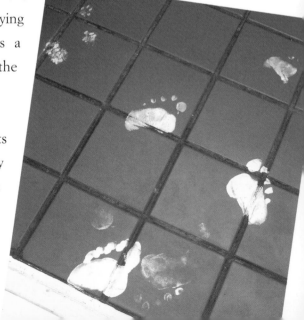

Drying Times Drying times of paints and varnishes are affected by such atmospheric conditions as humidity, the temperature of the room and the surface to which the product is applied. As a rough guide, allow about 20–30 minutes for acrylic varnish and water-based paints to become touch-dry. Oil-based paints and varnishes should be touch-dry in 2–3 hours and left overnight to become hard-dry before re-coating.

Coverage The covering power of paint and varnish depends on the type of paint used, how porous the surface is and the thickness of the coat. The side of the can will give the manufacturer's estimate.

Brushes Buy the best brushes you can afford — inferior ones won't last as long and can affect the finish. Decorator's brushes range in size from 1 inch (2.5cm) to 4 inches (10cm) and are useful for priming and for applying both oil- and water-based paints. Good-quality varnish brushes with hog's hair bristles give a smooth finish and can be used for glazes. Stencil brushes should also be natural bristle. Use small brushes for details and hand-painting.

Use separate brushes for materials with different bases — oil, water or resin — and always apply a new colour or material with a fresh brush, or one that has been well cleaned. Clean brushes used to apply oil-based products with white spirit, and remove water-based paints and varnishes with water. Clean brushes used for white polish with methylated spirits. The equipment section at the start of each project lists the types of brush you will need — it is not always necessary to buy the exact ones listed as some brushes can be adapted. A clean decorator's brush, for example, can be substituted for the wide varnish brush specified in most projects. However, if you are using oil-based polyurethane varnish to finish an effect created with water-based materials — or vice versa — remember to apply it with a fresh brush.

Water-based Paints	Type and use
Acrylic primer or convertor	Good, all-purpose primer made from acrylic polymers; also useful for priming laminated surfaces and vinyls. Not as thick as oil-based undercoat.
Emulsion paint	Standard, modern-day paint made from acrylic polymers and polyvinyl acetate (PVA) combined and dispersed in water to form an emulsion binder. Quick drying, available in matt or vinyl silk (see below). Not suitable for glaze work. Available in very thick, one-coat versions.
Vinyl silk (see above)	Unabsorbent so can be a used for glaze work. Higher content of PVA gives sheen. Quick drying but tends to be very thin, so more coats required. Can be washed and is tougher than matt emulsion.
Acrylic eggshell	Water-based version of traditional oil-based eggshell. Suitable for wood work. Very dense and sticky; dries to a soft sheen that is hard and very durable. Ideal as a base for oil and acrylic scumble glazes.
Acrylic gloss	Relatively new. Dries to a hard-wearing, glossy finish but is not as smooth as oil-based gloss; brushmarks do not level out as well as with oils.
Impasto or textured paint	Contemporary paint to create texture; an emulsion with added thickener and binder. Dries to a matt, chalky texture.
Woodwash	Specialist paint available from Paint Magic. Chalky, matt and opaque with added thickeners; can be burnished with wire wool and polished with wax to create a deep shine or diluted to use as a woodstain.

Oil-based Paint	Type and use
Undercoat	Thick, sticky, white primer for woodwork; also adheres well to plastic and metal. Flat, slightly chalky texture. Thick, opaque coverage fills small indentations in surface; can be tinted; good for adding to oil-based scumble glaze to make it more opaque and 'knock back' intense colours.
Eggshell	Great favourite for woodwork; also used as a base for oil glazes and for mixing into glazes. More fashionable apearance than gloss; dull sheen and tough, opaque coverage. Dries slowly and must be applied smoothly.
Gloss	Very durable, hard-wearing paint. High level of resin gives deep, gloss finish. Good surface preparation needed as gloss will highlight any unevenness in the surface.
Floor paint	High proportion of varnish makes it hard-wearing and water-resistant.

Waxes, Varnishes & Lacquers	Type and use
Beeswax	Soft, white wax from honeycombs. Can be softened with heat and mixed with pigments or artist's oil colours to stain wood or create specialist effects; also used for distressing effects.
Carnauba wax	One of the hardest waxes available; dark brown, can polish up to a very high shine for woodwork. Very high melting point. Comes from the Brazilian palm.
Liming wax	White wax; chalk (whiting) or white pigment can be added to produce liming and antiquing effects for hard woods, e.g. oak and ash.
Boot polish	Very versatile, household product. Ideal for polishing and antiquing freshly painted surfaces. Different colours.
Polyurethane varnish (matt, satin, gloss)	The most widely available of oil-based varnishes. Clear with a slight yellowing tinge. Slow drying, tough.
Yacht varnish	Extra-tough with high resistance to water, wear and tear. Yellows.
Acrylic varnish (matt, satin, gloss)	Water-based. White, opaque, with a pearly shimmer when wet; dries transparent. Matt is rarely completely flat. Extremely quick drying but does not achieve as smooth, flexible or hard-wearing a finish as oil-based varnishes.
Crackle glaze (crackle varnish)	Water-based. Causes water-based paints to split and reveal the surface underneath.
Craquelure	Two varnishes of different drying speeds that react to produce a cracked effect. Traditionally a water-based varnish was applied over an oil-based one; complete water-based versions are now available.
Shellac	Fast-drying, alcohol-based resinous varnish. Can be applied in multiple layers and sanded to super-fine, lacquer-like sheen; derived from the 'lac' beetle.

CLASSIC WHITE FLOOR

To prove that creating a beautiful floor can be utterly simple, we painted one with a couple of coats of standard oil-based white gloss paint. It is well worth while spending time and effort on preparing the floorboards as the paint will highlight any unevenness in the surface.

MATERIALS
patent 'knotting' sealant
white oil-based gloss paint
gloss acrylic varnish

EQUIPMENT
small brush or cloth for knotting sealant
hammer
3–4 inch (7.5–10cm) decorator's brush for paint
wide varnish brush

1 Seal knots in the floor with the knotting sealant to prevent sap leaking through and staining the paint. Make sure, too, that any nails standing proud are hammered flush.

2 Apply 2 coats of white oil-based gloss paint. Allow the first coat to dry before applying the second one.

3 Cover the floor with 2–3 coats of gloss acrylic varnish. Leave the first coat to dry before applying the second one.

This classic glossy white floor combined with primrose yellow walls, creates an airy, bright effect that would be particularly appropriate for a basement room that requires reflected light.

SCANDINAVIAN BLEACHED FLOOR Pale, bleached-looking floorboards immediately evoke the atmosphere of a cool, uncluttered Scandinavian interior. Subtle and understated, such a floor is ideal to complement a range of furnishing styles, from delicate antique painted furniture to stark modern pieces. The bleached look is also an excellent way of improving the look of characterless new pine floorboards, or of hiding some of the sins of older ones. There is something casual about the style which fits well with contemporary tastes for natural, rather than synthetic, materials and for products which respect the environment. A liming wax finish is optional, but adds sheen as well as extra pallor.

MATERIALS	EQUIPMENT
patent 'knotting' sealant	small brush or cloth for
pale grey matt emulsion	knotting sealant
paint (Driftwood	hammer
Woodwash)	equipment for mixing
matt acrylic varnish	paint and water
liming wax (optional)	3 inch (7.5cm) decorator's
	brush(es) for paint
	wide varnish brush
	soft cloths

The bleached floor is a perfect foil for this distressed, painted wooden chair. The walls of the room are a mixture of ochre and apricot colourwash, subtle enough not to overpower the floor, but rich enough to prevent the overall effect becoming cold.

1 Seal knots in the floorboards with knotting sealant. This will prevent excess sap in the knots leaking through and staining the final paint effect. Make sure, too, that any nails standing proud are hammered flush.

2 Mix 3–5 parts water to 1 part matt emulsion, according to the intensity of colour required. This may also be dictated by the colour of the floorboards you are painting. Lighter ones will require thinner coats than dark ones. Brush the paint out thinly over the bare boards following the grain. Leave to dry.

3

2

4

3 Cover the floor with 2–3 coats of matt acrylic varnish. Allow time for each coat to dry before applying the next one.

4 When the surface is hard-dry, apply a coat of liming wax, if you wish, with a soft cloth. Remove excess wax with a clean, dry, soft cloth. Buff to a low sheen.

SUBTLE CRACKLE-GLAZED FLOOR One young London designer recently used the crackle-glazed finish shown here over sheets of cheap, hardboard flooring to add discreet glamour on a shoestring to a svelte, deco-style interior done in natural colours. The effect was subtle but chic. It is an idea worth copying because the technique is simple, the materials inexpensive and the 'alligatored' finish adds texture to the functional floor covering. We liked his cool buff-on-white colour scheme, but any two water-based paint colours can be substituted.

To achieve a 'squared up' crackle, as here, simply brush the top coat of emulsion at right angles to the base coat. Make sure the crackle-glaze layer, sandwiched between the coats of emulsion, covers the surface evenly. It has a tacky consistency and needs to be brushed out carefully. The scale of 'crackling' depends on the thickness of the top emulsion — a thick coat gives bold cracks, a thin one creates an effect like 'crazing' on porcelain. Crackle glaze is activated by water so it is essential to seal the finished surface rapidly with a non-water-based varnish. We used quick-drying white polish for speed followed by two coats of tough varnish. You could use gloss acrylic or polyurethane varnish for heavy-duty protection.

Our neutral-toned, heavily distressed, crackled floor finish is very laid back, very contemporary. Low off-contrast colours look sophisticated (Warm White Woodwash), strong colours — blue on yellow, green on red, black on gold — have more impact. Choose whatever fits your style.

MATERIALS	EQUIPMENT
acrylic primer (use a fast-drying version)	3–4 inch (7.5–10cm) decorator's brush(es) for primer, paints and crackle glaze
white matt emulsion paint	
crackle glaze	
beige matt emulsion paint (Smoke Woodwash)	2 wide varnish brushes for white polish and varnish
white polish	
gloss acrylic or polyurethane varnish	

1 Prime your hardboard or plywood surface with acrylic primer and leave to dry.

2 Apply a covering coat of warm white matt emulsion and leave to dry.

3

3 Paint the crackle glaze over the base coat. Brush in one direction and make sure the whole surface is evenly covered. Leave to dry. After 1–2 minutes the glaze will seem to move. This is normal and will stop when the crackle glaze dries.

4 Paint the beige matt emulsion over the dried glaze, brushing at right angles to the warm white base coat. Load the brush with paint for big cracks and brush out firmly to cover, but *do not rebrush* after cracks appear (1–2 minutes) because this creates smears. Allow to dry.

5 Lightly touch in 'skips' or 'gaps' and leave to dry once again. Seal the entire surface with white polish. Leave to dry then apply 2 coats of protective acrylic or polyurethane varnish. Allow the first coat to dry completely before applying the second one.

4

DENIM-LOOK FLOOR The rugged good looks of everyone's favourite jeans — tough texture played off against deep, weathered blue colouring — make an unexpected showing underfoot as a painted floor treatment. This effect is best on a boarded floor, the grainier the better. Like its denim inspiration, it is a look at once classic and contemporary, to be played up or down depending on your furnishings. It makes a great background to country-style pieces, checks and rag rugs, but is equally at home in a shiny, high-tech kitchen. We love the denim indigo blue, but black, rust or caramel would all look good as a distressed top coat over a white base.

On small areas it is best, if effortful, to rub back the top coat by hand — wear heavy-duty household gloves while doing so. For larger floors either recruit family or friends to help, or cautiously rub back with a hand sander and fine-grade paper.

This could well be the trendiest floor finish of the late twentieth century — gutsy, colourful and unpretentious, with just a touch of swagger and a hint of wide open spaces. It's a great floor to scatter with kilim or ethnic rugs, but unexpectedly sexy (think of those Western heroines in denims and frilly, broderie anglaise blouses), counterpointing lace, linen and polished mahogany.

MATERIALS	EQUIPMENT
impasto or similarly textured paint	3–4 inch (7.5–10cm) decorator's brush(es)
off-white matt emulsion paint	impasto and emulsion paints
white wax household candles	heavy-duty household gloves
denim blue matt emulsion paint (Gitane and Midnight Woodwash)	medium- and fine-grade wire wool, or hand sander and fine-grade paper
matt polyurethane varnish	equipment for mixing varnish and white spirit
white spirit	wide varnish brush

1 Apply a base coat of impasto or textured paint to the floorboards, brushing in the direction of the woodgrain and making ridgy brushmarks. Leave to dry, then follow with 1 coat of off-white matt emulsion, brushed on in the same way as the impasto. Allow to dry.

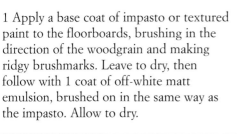

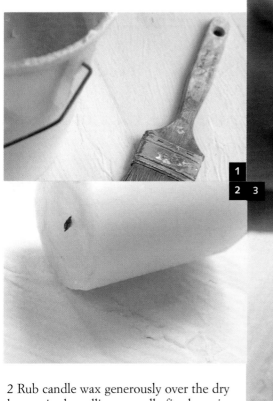

1
2 3

2 Rub candle wax generously over the dry base paint by rolling a candle firmly on its side in the direction of the grain. You should see flakes and smears of wax. The wax acts as a 'parting agent'.

4

3 Apply denim blue matt emulsion overall so that it covers well. Leave to dry.

4 Don your household gloves and use wire wool — medium grade followed by fine — to rub back the top coat, following the grain, until the white base coat surfaces in true denim fashion. Alternatively, try a hand sander but use it lightly so as not to scour the top coat away. Brush the finished floor clean, then apply at least 2 coats of polyurethane varnish. Thin the first one with 5 per cent of its volume of white spirit. Make sure each coat is dry before applying the next one.

FLORAL FLOOR TILES Stencilling walls and borders has become so fashionable over recent years that it needs little description. Stencil patterns on the floor, however, are less commonplace and can be seriously attractive. Here we have used simple, stylized flowers, a small violet plant with variations from the *Paintability Violet Bedroom* stencil set. But equally you could ·try to imitate a 'medieval' floor, with random stencils of scattered herbs; or a *trompe l'oeil* design that makes the room look as though it has a border of pebbles. The beauty of stencilling on hardboard or plywood squares is that the work can be done comfortably on the kitchen table rather than *in situ* on your hands and knees. The finished squares are glued down with a suitable adhesive and if the floor underneath is wood they can be further secured with fine panel pins. This method is also very useful for covering difficult or unsightly floors, but before you start, make sure the surface on which you will lay the squares is smooth and level (see page 24).

MATERIALS
18–24 inch (45–50cm) plywood or hardwood squares
acrylic primer
palest blue matt emulsion paint
artist's acrylic colours: blue-green, purple, raw umber, lemon yellow, crimson, white
eggshell acrylic or polyurethane varnish
wood adhesive or thixotropic contact adhesive

EQUIPMENT
medium-grade sandpaper
decorator's brush(es) for primer, paint and washy blue-green acrylic colour
masking tape
violet or other stencil designs (see above)
waxed paper plates for mixing acrylic colours
tracing paper, carbon (or transtrace) paper, pencil
stencil card
scalpel
stencil brush
wide varnish brush

fine panel pins and hammer (for wood base)

Pretty as painted china, this finished floor has come a long way from its humble beginnings. It could transform a drab bathroom or bedroom or, with a change of pattern and colours, add oomph to a child's bedroom or create a masculine study.

1 Measure and square up your room and work out how many squares you will need (see page 26). Have these — and any odd shapes needed to fit round pipes or fill gaps on floor plans — cut to size. It may be quicker to cut the irregular shapes yourself with a jigsaw or fretsaw.

2 Smooth the cut edges of the squares with sandpaper, then prime the squares with the acrylic primer. Remember to include the overlaps around the edges. Allow to dry, then cover each square with a coat of pale blue matt emulsion. Leave to dry.

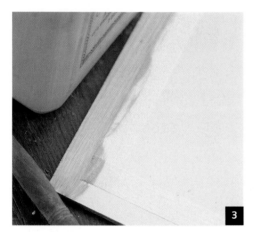

3

3 To make sure the borders to the squares are neat, run masking tape approximately $^3/_4$–1 inch (2–2.5cm) inside the cut edges. Mix the blue-green acrylic colour with water to make a washy colour, then paint this to the edges of the squares. Remember to include the overlaps, as in Step 2. Allow to dry, then peel off the tape.

4 Trace the violet stencil designs with tracing paper, then enlarge them on a photocopier. Use carbon paper to transfer them to stencil card. Outline the designs in pencil, then cut out stencils with the scalpel, changing the blade frequently.

5 Try different arrangements of stencils *in situ*. Each square can be a repeat or randomly arranged as here. When you are happy with the pattern, secure the stencils to the squares with tabs of masking tape. Apply the acrylic colours with an almost dry stencil brush (rub it on paper first to remove moisture) and a scrubbing action. Vary the colours from time to time over the squares.

6 When all the squares are finished and dry, varnish them with 2–3 coats of acrylic or polyurethane varnish. Remember to include the overlaps as before. Allow each coat to dry before applying the next one.

7 Starting in the middle of the room, and following the method outlined on page 27, stick the stencilled squares onto the floor. Use wood adhesive on wood, contact adhesive on concrete. Fine panel pins whacked in on the 4 corners of each square give extra durability on a wood base.

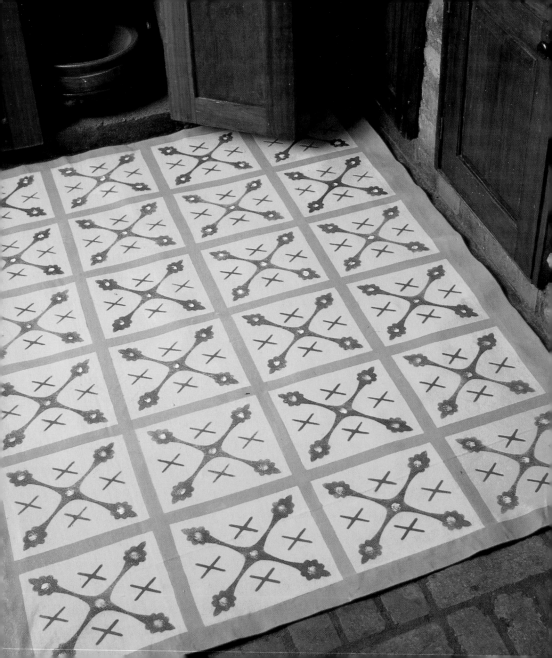

FLOOR CLOTH: HOMAGE TO THE NINETEENTH CENTURY

Floor cloths were immensely popular in the nineteenth century before the invention of linoleum made them obsolete. Here we have designed what might have been a typical floor cloth of the period, using the kind of simple, classical design in a limited palette of colours that was fashionable for ordinary houses. Our version makes use of modern techniques to speed up the drying process — the originals were painted with oil colours and left to dry for weeks on end. It is well worth expending effort and time to produce this floor cloth as it is both authentic for a period room and portable — it can be rolled up and taken to a new home in the future. If you do decide to transport it, treat it carefully and wrap it around a cylinder because the surface can crack.

The finished floorcloth, thrown down over a brick kitchen floor, immediately evokes a late-eighteenth or nineteenth-century interior. The cloth is hard-wearing and waterproof, ideal for a kitchen or bathroom, and has a rich appearance lacking in its modern equivalents.

MATERIALS	EQUIPMENT
stencil paints: pinky yellow, leaf green red, brick or terracotta, white	stencil pattern (see page 91)
canvas or cotton duck in 1 complete width (no seams), ironed flat	tracing paper, carbon (or transtrace) paper, pencil
white polish	stencil card
matt polyurethane varnish	scalpel
	strong cardboard
	masking tape
	stencil brush
	artist's small brush for details
	2 wide varnish brushes for white polish and varnish

1 Trace the stencil pattern with tracing paper, then enlarge it on a photocopier. Use transtrace or carbon paper to transfer it to stencil card. Outline the pattern in pencil, then cut out the stencil with a scalpel, changing the blade frequently.

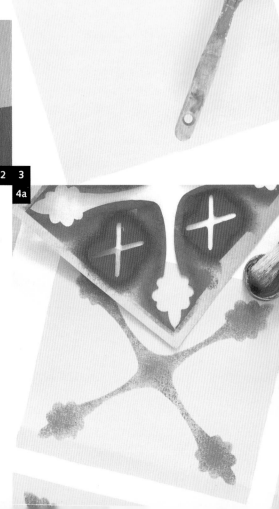

2 3
4a

2 Use the scalpel to cut an 8 × 9 inch (20 × 23cm) rectangle from the cardboard, then use this template to mark out squares on the canvas or cotton duck in pencil. Leave a 1 inch (2.5cm) margin between each square and a 1¹/₂ inch (4cm) border around the cloth.

3 Sectioning off the squares with masking tape as you work, paint each square with the pinky yellow stencil paint. Allow to dry.

4 Fix the stencil over each square in turn using pieces of masking tape. Stencil the main crosses with the leaf green stencil paint, and the 4 smaller crosses with red.

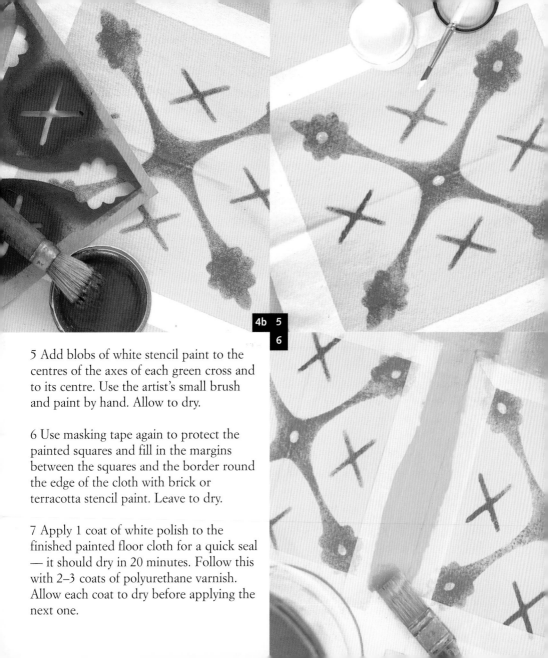

4b **5**
6

5 Add blobs of white stencil paint to the centres of the axes of each green cross and to its centre. Use the artist's small brush and paint by hand. Allow to dry.

6 Use masking tape again to protect the painted squares and fill in the margins between the squares and the border round the edge of the cloth with brick or terracotta stencil paint. Leave to dry.

7 Apply 1 coat of white polish to the finished painted floor cloth for a quick seal — it should dry in 20 minutes. Follow this with 2–3 coats of polyurethane varnish. Allow each coat to dry before applying the next one.

FAUX PARQUETRY FLOOR

Parquetry floors using a variety of indigenous and more exotic woods were introduced into Britain in the mid-seventeenth century. The most frequently laid designs were formal and classical like the one we imitate in this project. Cutting and laying parquetry is an extremely skilled, expensive and time-consuming task, not realistically manageable by the average home decorator. An imitation, using paints to copy the colours of woods, is comparatively easy to achieve, and surprisingly difficult to distinguish from the real thing at first, and even second, glance. The effect will look best on a floor surface of real boards, either old or brand-new. The secret of success lies with careful drawing up of the floor so that the painted lines are as clear as razor-cut wood might be.

MATERIALS
artist's acrylic colours:
  raw umber, burnt
  umber
matt or gloss
  polyurethane varnish

EQUIPMENT
metal ruler and pencil
scalpel
equipment for mixing
  acrylic colours and
  water
piece of wood
decorator's brush(es) for
  acrylic colours
wide varnish brush

The floor looks convincingly like parquetry, and shows how the knots in new floorboards have coloured up attractively with the application of tinted varnish. The gilded footstool gives an indication of how authentically seventeenth- or eighteenth-century a room treated in this way can appear: elegant, tasteful and posh enough to hold its own against heirloom pieces.

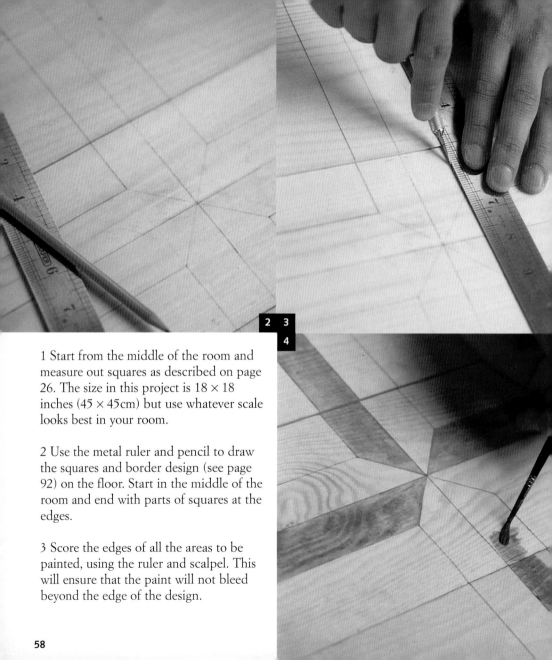

2 3
4

1 Start from the middle of the room and measure out squares as described on page 26. The size in this project is 18 × 18 inches (45 × 45cm) but use whatever scale looks best in your room.

2 Use the metal ruler and pencil to draw the squares and border design (see page 92) on the floor. Start in the middle of the room and end with parts of squares at the edges.

3 Score the edges of all the areas to be painted, using the ruler and scalpel. This will ensure that the paint will not bleed beyond the edge of the design.

5

6

4 Mix a little raw umber acrylic colour with water. Test its density on a piece of wood. It should contain enough raw umber to cover, but remain transparent enough to give the effect of woodstain. Paint the mixture onto alternate parts of the design, leaving a windmill star in the corners of the squares as shown.

5 Mix the burnt umber acrylic colour with water in the same manner as the raw umber, and complete the unpainted parts.

6 When the floor is completely dry, paint polyurethane varnish over the entire surface to seal it. Tint the varnish with a little raw umber if the floorboards are too starkly new in appearance.

GINGHAM-LOOK FLOOR   We came across a gingham-effect floor in an American magazine and found it fresh and attractive. The instructions for achieving it were complicated, and we were sure that the same idea could be achieved much more simply. Effectively, all we had to do was paint a criss-cross of stripes across the room using a transparent tinted paint glaze which would intensify on the squares where the stripes crossed. Mixing the scumble to precisely the right colour and density was the only difficult part of the procedure. Our starting-point was a classic white floor: see the project on page 35 for instructions on how to prepare this.

The finished floor gives a marvellous effect of gingham material, as light and airy as a summer dress. It looks particularly good in this room, which opens through French windows onto a patio and garden. The green we have used here seems to pull some of the foliage into the house, making a lovely 'garden room'.

MATERIALS
artist's oil colours:
   cadmium yellow,
   Prussian blue
oil scumble glaze
white spirit
Terebine drier
gloss polyurethane
varnish

EQUIPMENT
thick paper and scissors
tailor's chalk or oil-based
   pastel crayon in a
   colour similar to the
   paint
equipment for mixing oil
   colours, scumble
   glaze and white spirit
white-painted plank
masking tape
decorator's brush for
   scumble-glaze
   mixture

1 Cut strips of paper to the width of your stripes — ours were 11 inches (28cm) wide. You may want to experiment by cutting different widths of paper to see which look best in your room: a larger room can accommodate wider stripes than a small one.

2 Start with a cross in the centre of the room (see page 26) and use the stripe templates to mark out the lines of the stripes with oil crayon matching the intended stripe colour.

3 Mix the cadmium yellow and Prussian blue oil colours (45 per cent yellow to 55 per cent blue) into the scumble glaze and add enough white spirit to thin the mixture. You will need approximately 2 tubes of colour and $^{1}/_{2}$ pint (300ml) of turpentine or white spirit for every $3^{1}/_{2}$ pints (2 litres) of scumble glaze. Add a little Terebine drier to speed up the slow-drying oil mixture so that the floor does not have to be left untouched for too long.

4 Test the colour and effect of the scumble-glaze mixture on a white-painted plank and adjust the proportions of scumble glaze and white spirit if necessary.

5 Mask off the vertical stripes with masking tape and brush on the coloured glaze. Do not go back over painted areas, but leave distressed-looking brush strokes. Leave to dry for 4–6 hours in warm conditions, overnight if possible.

6 When the vertical stripes are completely dry, remove the masking tape and apply new masking tape at the edges of the horizontal stripes. Paint these as in Step 5, brushing straight over the vertical stripes at the crossing points so that the glaze is darker in these squares.

7 Leave the floor to dry overnight and then apply a coat of polyurethane varnish to seal the paint effect. Leave until hard-dry, then apply a second coat of varnish.

6

5

MODERN MOSAIC FLOOR

Thousands of years later, the dedicated are still at it, creating original mosaics on floors — a systematic and time-consuming task which nevertheless results in a uniquely patterned and uniquely durable surface. The mosaic design shown here is inspired by a floor design by the designer Lloyd Farmar (himself inspired by Matisse), who used this fish motif in a bathroom. The floor should be solid — concrete is ideal, as is hardboard. Use a cement-based adhesive to fix the mosaic pieces to a concrete surface, and add a flexible additive to this if your base is hardboard or wood — follow the manufacturer's instructions. The 'smalti' mosaic pieces are made of glass and can be bought in 'sheets' of different colours. The brown paper backing should be soaked off before use or, if large areas are to be covered in one colour, applied in one piece with the backing paper intact. This can be removed once the smalti have adhered firmly to the floor.

Anything more complex than a simple grid will require you to cut mosaic pieces to fit for flow and dynamism. You should wear plastic goggles when doing this, and gloves too when removing grout from the mosaic.

MATERIALS	EQUIPMENT	
tesserae or smalti mosaic pieces in appropriate colours	fish motif or other motif of your own design	equipment for mixing and applying hydrochloric acid and water
cement-based adhesive (X7 by Arduit) for concrete surface; plus flexible additive for hardboard or wood base	tracing paper, carbon paper, pencil hardened steel, titanium-tipped nippers	
tile grout	plastic goggles and gloves	
hydrochloric acid (available from chemists)	spatula wire wool synthetic household sponge	

Once fully dry, the floor mosaic is even and secure, there for years to come and free of any particular cleaning problems. The juxtaposition of mosaic pieces of slightly varying shades adds to the lightness and naturalness of the finished effect.

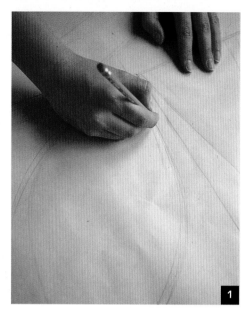

1 Design your own motif, or trace a design from this book, enlarge it on a photocopier and use carbon paper to transfer the design onto your surface.

2 Most of the mosaic pieces will need cutting in order to follow the curves and shapes of our free-form 'Matisse-inspired' design. Simply fit each piece into the nippers and squeeze the handles firmly. Don your plastic goggles to do this. Keep offcuts to fill small spaces in the design.

3 Apply the cement-based adhesive, mixed with the additive if necessary, to the floor surface within the drawn lines. Now fix the pieces of smalti or tesserae onto the adhesive. If they have bevelled edges, place the smaller surface downwards. The random shapes must be close together, in pleasing colour combinations, but need not abut each other. Let the adhesive dry hard.

4 Use the spatula to work the tile grout over the surface of the mosaic. All the gaps between the cut pieces must be filled in to give a flush surface. Leave to dry for about 30 minutes.

5 Rub back the surface with wire wool, then clean it off with a wet sponge. To remove any grout still adhering to the dried mosaic, mix 1 part hydrochloric acid with 15 parts water and brush over the floor – wear protective gloves. The solution will fizz as it works. Finally, rinse the acid off with lots of clean water.

3a 3b
4   5

STENCILLED MOSAIC FLOOR

If the real thing really is too much work — or too expensive — a stencilled mosaic can be extraordinarily effective, especially when applied to a concrete floor, which provides the most convincing background. It is also an inspired way of treating an uneven or damaged surface that is better hidden: the irregularities will seem to be part of the design rather than deficiencies. The classical motifs in this project give the floor the look of a Roman pavement, and could be used for a room such as a hallway which would traditionally have had a stone floor. You could create your own stencil patterns using tracings of other Roman mosaics.

MATERIALS	EQUIPMENT
stone-coloured matt emulsion paint	stencil design (see page 93)
artist's acrylic colours: raw umber, sienna, yellow ochre	tracing paper, carbon paper, pencil
white matt emulsion paint	stencil card
matt polyurethane varnish	scalpel
	decorator's brush for stone-coloured paint
	equipment for mixing white paint and acrylic colours
	two stencil brushes: 1 large, 1 medium
	wide varnish brush

The finished floor looks astonishingly authentic, given the fact that it is achieved entirely with paint. Here the border stencil has been applied in a mixture of darker shades to provide a strong pattern around the edges of the room, and the remaining area is stencilled in stone colours. The room would also look effective just with the border, perhaps with the rest of the room painted one neutral colour to imitate stone.

4 Tint some white matt emulsion with raw umber and raw sienna to make pinky brown, and with yellow ochre and raw umber to create dirty yellow. Use these mixtures to stipple randomly through the stencil for a variegated marble/stone finish.

5 Apply 3 coats of polyurethane varnish to protect the stencilled paints. Allow each coat to dry before applying the next one.

1 Trace the stencil design for the border with tracing paper, then enlarge it on a photocopier and use carbon paper to transfer it onto stencil card. Outline the design in pencil then cut out the stencil using a scalpel. Work out your own arrangement of 'tile' shapes to make a stencil for the main part of the floor.

2 Paint the entire floor surface with stone-coloured matt emulsion. Leave to dry.

3 Mix enough raw sienna acrylic colour into the white matt emulsion to make a warm white. Then use the stencil brushes and mixture to stipple the complete design over the base colour, a section at a time.

4

CHEQUERBOARD FLOOR

In the seventeenth century, the floors of northern European houses of quality were characteristically tiled with a chequerboard pattern of black and white, or blue-grey and white, stone or slate. The style is familiar from Dutch and Flemish paintings of interiors, where the floors add calm and grandeur to modest rooms. The same pattern is frequently laid in stone today, but for a less expensive finish, or for the floor of an upper-storey room which may not be able to take the weight, a chequerboard effect can be painted straight onto floorboards. We chose grey-green squares rather than the more dramatic black for the living room shown here, and dulled down the white paint to increase the subtlety of the effect.

MATERIALS	EQUIPMENT
off-white matt emulsion paint	strong cardboard
grey-green matt emulsion paint (Slate Woodwash)	equipment for mixing colours
matt or gloss polyurethane or acrylic varnish	decorator's brush(es) for paints
	pencil
	lots of masking tape
	wide varnish brush

The finished chequerboard floor looks good here with crisp contemporary furniture, but would also complement a more traditional room. In either case, choose a 'dirty white' so that the effect is not too stark and new looking; rather, it should look as though this particular floor was always meant to be in place.

3a 3b
3c

1 Measure up your room and decide on the size of squares that will look most effective. We settled on 20 × 20 inches (50 × 50cm). Cut a square template from the cardboard.

2 Paint over the boards with a good covering coat of the mixture and leave to dry. Two coats may be needed for opacity.

3 Starting at the centre of the room (see page 26), use the template and a pencil to draw squares on the floor. Mask off all the squares to be painted with masking tape.

4 Paint the grey-green emulsion onto the masked off squares. Leave to dry and then remove the masking tape.

5 Seal the painted floor with 3 coats of polyurethane varnish, or acrylic varnish if you are worried about yellowing over time. Whichever type you decide on, allow each coat to dry before applying the next one.

COMBED FLOOR Once the painting of straightforward alternate chequerboard squares has been mastered, the process can be taken one stage further with these 'combed' squares. The finished effect is reminiscent of stripy pink Italian marble with its warm, rosy glow and grainy texture. Obviously, the same technique can be used in different colours, to imitate other types of marble or simply to create a pleasantly textured, non-naturalistic effect with a brighter palette. This effect is ideal for a floor covered with hardboard or plywood, both of which provide a smooth surface. It will not be easy to achieve as good a result with floorboards, particularly if the planks are old and uneven.

MATERIALS	EQUIPMENT
cream matt emulsion paint (Aubusson Cream)	strong cardboard
	decorator's brush(es) for paints and glaze mixture
red matt emulsion paint (Barn Red Woodwash)	pencil
acrylic scumble glaze	masking tape
matt or gloss polyurethane varnish	scalpel
	equipment for mixing red matt emulsion and acrylic scumble glaze
	flexible rubber comb
	cotton rags
	wide varnish brush

The finished floor gives a warm, antiqued feel to a small study, bringing instant character to a brand-new house. There is no indication that the surface is a cheap wood substitute.

1 Following the instructions in Step 1 of the previous project, cut out a cardboard template in your desired size of square.

2 Paint the entire surface of the floor with cream matt emulsion. Leave to dry.

3 Starting at the centre of the room (see page 26), use the template and a pencil to draw squares on the floor. Apply masking tape to define the edges of squares.

4 Alternate squares will be combed through in opposite directions. Cut into the masking tape crosses with the scalpel to reveal the corners of the squares that will be combed in one direction.

5 Mix the red matt emulsion and acrylic scumble glaze in a 50:50 ratio. The result will be a liquid but viscous mixture.

6 Apply a thin coat of the glaze mixture to the squares you have marked with a scalpel, and then comb through it in one direction with the rubber comb. Wipe the comb clean with water and a cotton rag after completing each square. Allow all the squares to dry.

7 Remove the masking tape from the dried squares and prepare the remaining squares —which will be combed in the opposite direction — as in Steps 3 and 4. Paint the glaze mixture over these squares and comb them as in Step 6. Leave to dry, then remove the masking tape.

8 Seal the floor with 2–3 coats of polyurethane varnish. Allow each coat to dry before applying the next one.

PATCHWORK TILE DOORSTEP Moving to the outside of the house, we decided to treat a doorstep to its own funky and simple mosaic to provide something altogether more interesting and lively than the original bare concrete. This sort of treatment is traditionally suggested as a way of using up old, broken tiles. If you have some, or are removing tiles from other parts of the house, or can acquire broken bits from a manufacturer, this is ideal; if not, don't feel too guilty about buying a small number of unbroken seconds and smashing them up yourself. Use a small hammer and don't break them too small. Wear plastic goggles while smashing or cover the tiles with newspaper. We used a variety of colours in muted shades for our doorstep, to give a kaleidoscopic effect. We used a variety of colours in muted shades for our doorstep, to give a kaleidoscopic effect.

MATERIALS	EQUIPMENT
cement-based adhesive (such as X7 by Arduit)	small trowel or palette knife
tile grout	small hammer and plastic goggles and
broken tiles	newspaper, or
hydrochloric acid (available from hardware stores)	hardened steel, titanium-tipped nippers
	rubber tile-scraper
	damp cloth

This is the simplest possible piece of mosaic art — a random pattern achieved on a very small area. Even so, it makes a very welcoming threshold for what would otherwise be an unremarkable doorway, and introduces life and colour to an area normally completely lacking in decoration.

3 Place the pieces of tile side-by-side on the doorstep and press them down firmly into the adhesive. Allow the adhesive to dry hard, but scrape off excess first.

4 Apply grout over entire surface with a spatula, scraping off the excess with a rubber tile scraper. Let dry hard – about 30 minutes – then go over again with the spatula to clear the surface. Wipe with a damp cloth.

1 Break up the tiles into suitable sizes using a hammer, as described above, or cut the pieces into more convenient shapes using the nippers — simply fit the piece into them and squeeze the handles firmly.

2 Apply a thick layer of cement-based adhesive to the doorstep with trowel or palette knife. Do this as you go, tiling a section at a time.

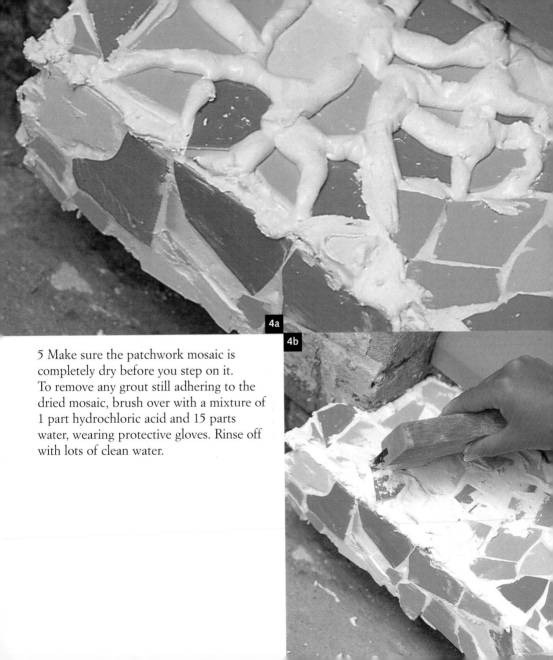

4a

4b

5 Make sure the patchwork mosaic is completely dry before you step on it. To remove any grout still adhering to the dried mosaic, brush over with a mixture of 1 part hydrochloric acid and 15 parts water, wearing protective gloves. Rinse off with lots of clean water.

MAINTENANCE & CLEANING

In 1760, Hannah Glasse published her *Servant's Directory or Housekeeper's Companion*, in which she described methods of floor cleaning to be used by servants in wealthy middle-class households like her own. Cleaning may remain a chore today, but it was a major operation and a spur to ingenuity and invention in past centuries.

The projects in this book reproduce some of the techniques and materials that have traditionally been used to decorate floors, and the old cleaning methods therefore remain pertinent – and can be noted and adapted, if not actually copied to the letter. They are particularly relevant in an age where people are aware of the environmental problems caused by the over-use of chemicals and synthetic cleaning agents, and the waste of energy entailed by multifarious household appliances. This applies especially to floors. Hygiene is less important on an area that is constantly trodden with outside shoes than it is on kitchen surfaces where food is prepared. In addition, hard floor surfaces do not require a vacuum cleaner. You are better off using an old-fashioned broom and string mop.

Glasse instructs that carpets should be swept clean with a broom. Even better is to turn the carpet upside-down for a few days so that the dust is 'beaten' out of it by the tread of feet on the reverse side: the dust can be swept off the floor underneath once the carpet is ready to be turned back. This is a handy hint even now for anyone who is reluctant to bother with vacuuming or keen to save resources.

'Dry' cleaning was obviously necessary when water was not readily and constantly available on tap, and Glasse suggests that for hard floors the housekeeper '...take some Sand, pretty damp, but not too wet, and strew all over the Room, throwing it out of your Hand hard, and it will fly about the Floor and lick up all the Dust and Flew.' It all sounds quite fun by boring twentieth-century cleaning standards, but is probably not a method that will be readily used. Nevertheless, it is worth noting that damp sand will absorb dust, and that it has the mild abrasive properties needed on many hard surfaces. Glasse's advice for stained floorboards is that they should be treated with ox gall and left overnight, then scoured with hot ashes and again with sand.

Glasse's near-contemporary, Susanna Whatman, produced a *Housekeeping Book* between 1776 and 1800. She distrusted wetting floors, which she felt led to damp and to 'vapours' a word feared in the eighteenth century as synonymous with potential diseases, from the ague to consumption, which were erroneously thought to be transmitted by such auras. Wetting floors, she says, should be reserved for once-a-year spring cleaning and, in any case, soap was expensive and tended to leave a white deposit on the surfaces it was supposed to be restoring. Green herbs, dry-brushed and rubbed into the floor, then swept off, produced a sweet-smelling alternative. Tansy, mint, balm and fennel were her aromatic suggestions. Floor cloths should be swept and then wiped with a flannel. When all the dust and spots were removed, they should be rubbed with a waxed flannel, then a dry plain one. Too much wax, however, would make them slippery. Washing floor cloths with milk would give a beautiful, non-slip surface. A milk wash was also recommended for slate floors and quarry tiles. Glasse was slightly less industrious when it came to floor cloths, suggesting that, 'if not too dirtied, a floorcloth may be kept clean by wiping it with a damp cloth, and afterwards rubbing it with a dry cloth, and then with a brush till it shines.' Stone and brick floors were sometimes sealed with isingglass.

According to Whatman, hard floors could be treated with sand alone for a dry rub, sand and fuller's earth (a dull green clay used in cloth-making and well known for its cleaning properties) for wet scouring. This is where the sandman came in, transporting sand and other products for cleaning to areas of the country where they were not naturally available. Barely damp tea leaves could be used to clean carpets; they were sprinkled on and brushed off with a stiff broom. The maintenance of her floors was a source of much anxiety — even obsession — for Whatman, who exhorted in a letter home to her housekeeper in 1799: 'but above all I beg the floors of those two rooms may not be wetted while I am absent, at least not till I mention it.' No greater, life-threatening sin, it seems, could possibly be committed by her housekeeping staff. Her approach may seem Draconian, but in fact standards of cleanliness varied widely in the eighteenth century.

Today we have abundant water on tap, and are all too used to splashing it about without a second thought. It is our main cleaning material, however combined or applied, and there is no denying its efficacy. Very many hard-surface floors can be cleaned with water alone, or water mixed with soap or detergents of varying severity. It is worth bearing in mind that strong detergents will gradually damage most surfaces, and are particularly unkind to paint, although protective varnishes, applied as we suggest in our projects, offer an impressive defence.

Even so, different floor surfaces are best taken care of with different methods of cleaning and different techniques should certainly be used to restore them. The sections following provide a few hints on how to give your underfoot territory long and handsome life.

Whatever the hard-floor surface, bear in mind Susanna Whatman's concern about too much water. Water will damage almost any floor if it has the time to lie there and seep through tiny cracks. To 'beg the floors not be wetted' should be at the back of the mind in the twentieth century, just as it was in the eighteenth.

Encaustic Tiles

Many existing nineteenth- and early twentieth-century houses still have encaustic floor tiles in place, in varying degrees of repair. They are often in entrance hallways and are well worth restoring and preserving. The chances are that they will have been laid to fit closely together without grouting. Over the years, dirt and grit may have eased itself into the gaps and loosened the tiles. In this case they need to be carefully lifted – make sure you remember which tile goes where – and the area beneath cleaned. Use a thin layer of tile cement when replacing them. When the cement is dry, wipe the tiles over with grout to make sure they are secure.

If the old tiles are simply dirty, they can be cleaned with white spirit diluted with water. Apply the mixture with a scouring pad (not wire wool, which will damage the surface), and wash it off with clean water. It is inadvisable to use a sealant on a tile floor as it will prevent any damp from the floor evaporating, and the tiles underneath the seal will gradually rot. Instead, polish the tiles to a perfumed shine with beeswax, applied with a soft cloth.

Stone Floors

The most basic care is to sweep stone floors regularly. Wash them when necessary with mild soap and water – the French use *Savon de Marseille*, a gentle, olive-oil-based product. An untreated stone floor will stain, so it is best to protect it with a recommended silicone-based sealant. Scratches will appear, but should be enjoyed as part of the patina, more attractive than completely unmarked stone. In the eighteenth century, stone floors were usually cleaned with sand and water.

If flagstones are particularly old or damaged, or have been painted over, they can be dug up comparatively easily, professionally cleaned and then relaid.

Wooden Floors

As we have seen, in previous centuries parquet and timber-boarded floors were first waxed and polished, then kept clean by sweeping and by rubbing with aromatic herbs. Today they can, of course, still be swept and spills on a floor can be mopped up with water. A wooden floor should never be allowed to get soaking wet as the finish, especially a waxed one, will quickly deteriorate. If the wood becomes really worn and dull, it can be restored by sanding lightly by hand and re-applying the varnish, wax or oil top coat.

An old wooden floor must remain free of woodworm and rot, and boards must be properly nailed down. Proprietary woodfillers can be used to fill small holes, and wedges of wood inserted into larger gaps.

Brick

Bricks are most commonly found in passageways and kitchens, two of the most frequently used areas of the house, and are subject to a lot of wear and tear, grease and spills. In a kitchen, particularly, they should be treated with a silicone-based sealant. If they are untreated they will absorb liquid and oils and be almost impossible to clean.

Once sealed, they can be washed with water, with detergent solutions if necessary, and, of course, simply swept clean.

Painted Floors

The painted-floor projects in this book are finished with a number of coats of oil-based polyurethane or water-based acrylic varnish to protect the effects underneath from damage. A polyurethane surface can be cleaned with the usual soap and water or detergent and water, but it is well worth noting that you will probably be able to clean it quite satisfactorily without using detergents.

Acrylic varnish is more vulnerable to cleaning agents, and simple, mild soap and water is preferable to vicious household detergents.

Vinyl, Linoleum, Cork Tiles, etc

These surfaces are particularly hard-wearing, and can be swept and washed without much fuss or bother. Again, go easy on detergents or solvents, which may remove some of the colour. Most cork tiles are covered with a coat of polyurethane varnish, but they look richer if they are finished off instead with beeswax.

FURTHER READING

Ayres, James, *The Shell Book of the Home in Britain*, 1981

Barnard, Nicholas, *Arts and Crafts of India*, 1993

Beard, Geoffrey, *The National Trust Book of the English House Interior*, 1990

Davidson, Caroline, *A Woman's Work is Never Done: A History of Housework in the British Isles 1650-1950*, 1986

Eastlake, Charles, *Hints on Household Taste*, 1878 (ed. Gloag, John, 1969)

Edis, Robert, *The Decoration and Furniture of Town Houses*, 1881

Furnival, W. J., *Leadless Decorative Tiles*, 1904

Gilbert, Christopher, et al, *Country House Floors 1660-1850*, exhibition catalogue, Temple Newsam, Leeds, 1987

Glasse, Hannah, *The Servant's Directory or Housekeeper's Companion*, 1760

Grey, Edwin, *Cottage Life in a Hertfordshire Village: How the Agricultural Labourer Lived and Fared in the late 60s and the 70s*, 1935

Innes, Jocasta, *The New Decorator's Handbook*, 1995

Innes, Jocasta, *The New Paint Magic*, 1992

Innes, Jocasta, and Walton, Stewart, *Paintability Violet Bedroom* (stencil kit), 1989

Johnson, Peter, *Romano-British Mosaics*, 1982

Leland, C. G., *The Minor Arts*, 1880

Meader, R. F. W., *Illustrated Guide to Shaker Furniture*, 1972

Praz, Mario, *An Illustrated History of Interior Decoration*, 1964

Rowntree, Seebohm, *How the Labourer Lives*, 1913

Service, Alistair, *Edwardian Interiors*, 1982

Webster, Thomas, *Encyclopaedia of Domestic Economy*, 1844

Whatman, Susanna, *The Housekeeping Book of Susanna Whatman*, *1776-1800*, reprinted 1987

Zahle, Erik, *Scandinavian Domestic Design*, 1963

Stencil template for Floor Cloth (page 54)

Template for Faux Parquetry border design (page 58)

Stencil template for Stencilled Mosaic border (page 69)

PAINT MAGIC SHOPS

Paint Magic offers a complete range of decorative paints, traditional ingredients, brushes, stencils and books. Each branch also offers weekly courses in decorative paint techniques.

PAINT MAGIC MAIL ORDER
79 Shepperton Road
Islington, London
N1 3DF
United Kingdom
tel (0171) 226 4420 fax (0171) 226 7760

UNITED KINGDOM

PAINT MAGIC ARUNDEL
26 The High Street
Arundel, West Sussex BN18 9AB
tel (01903) 883653 fax (01903) 884367

PAINT MAGIC BELFAST
59 The High Street
Holywood, County Down BT18 9AQ
tel (01232) 421881 fax (01232) 421823

PAINT MAGIC GUILDFORD
3 Chapel Street
Guildford, Surrey GU1 3UH
tel (01483) 306072

PAINT MAGIC ISLINGTON
34 Cross Street
Islington, London N1 2BG
tel (0171) 359 4441 fax (0171) 359 1833

PAINT MAGIC NOTTING HILL
5 Elgin Crescent
Notting Hill Gate, London W11 2JA
tel (0171) 792 8012 fax (0171) 727 0207

PAINT MAGIC RICHMOND
116 Sheen Road
Richmond, Surrey TW9 1UR
tel (0181) 940 9799 fax (0181) 332 7503

UNITED STATES

Paint Magic products are stocked by Pottery Barn branches across the United States. For details of your nearest stockist, call Pottery Barn customer service (800) 922 9934, or write to:

POTTERY BARN MAIL ORDER DEPARTMENT
P.O. Box 7044
San Francisco, CA 94120-7044
tel (415) 983 9887

CANADA

PAINT MAGIC CALGARY
101, 1019 # 17th Avenue SW
Calgary, Alberta T2T 0A7
tel (403) 245 6866 fax (403) 244 2471

ISRAEL

PAINT MAGIC TEL AVIV
255 Dijengoff Street
Tel Aviv 63117
tel (972) 3605 2476 fax (972) 3544 5710

SINGAPORE

PAINT MAGIC SINGAPORE
Seik Yee Paint Shop
30 Watten Rise
Singapore 1128
tel (65) 463 1982 fax (65) 463 1982

FURTHER DETAILS

There are more Paint Magic shops opening worldwide in the near future. Please call or write for our catalogue, price list, Design and Decoration Service and details of the latest shop to open near you.

PAINT MAGIC HEAD OFFICE
77 Shepperton Road
Islington, London N1 3DF
United Kingdom
tel (44) (0)171 354 9696 fax (44) (0)171 226 7760

First United States Edition

First published in Great Britain by Macmillan, an imprint of Macmillan Publishers Limited

ISBN 0-8212-2452-2

Library of Congress Catalog Card Number 97-71298

Bulfinch Press is an imprint and trademark of Little, Brown and Company (Inc.)
Published simultaneously in Canada by Little, Brown & Company (Canada) Limited.

Series Origination: Jocasta Innes
Text and Research: Judy Spours

Design: Hammond Hammond

Original Photography:
Marie-Louise Avery, Sue Baker

ACKNOWLEDGEMENTS
Special thanks go to Amtico (01203 861400), pioneers of high-tech and designer floor finishes, Agora London (0181 946 2593), specialists in hardwood floors using fine reclaimed timbers and historic designs, and to the designer Tim Coppard, for their provision of photographs for the introductory section. Thanks also go to Paint Magic Islington for use of their patchwork tile doorstep, and Paint Magic Richmond for their stencilled mosaic floor.

Jocasta Innes also wishes to thank:
Project Manager: Sarah Curran
Assistants: Tim Tari, Sammy Dent
Senior Commissioning Editor for
Boxtree/Macmillan: Gordon Scott Wise
Editor: Tessa Clark

PICTURE CREDITS
Marie-Louise Avery 1, 38-9, 42-3, 46-7, 50-1, 54-5, 56, 58-9, 62-3, 65, 66-7, 70-1, 74-5, 78-9; Sue Baker 2, 3 (bottom), 17, 20, 28, 29, 30, 34, 37, 40, 44, 49, 52, 57, 60, 68, 72, 77, 80, 82-3, 87, 88 (left), 89 (left); Agora London 14; Amtico 6, 22, 23, 89 (right); Tim Coppard/ David George 5, 8 (bottom), 9; Jocasta Innes 3 (top), 7, 8 (top), 12, 16; Paint Magic 13, 26, 88 (right), 95.

Printed in Italy